The Eucalypts

poems by

Casey Elizabeth Newbegin

The Eucalypts

Copyright © 2025 by Casey Elizabeth Newbegin

ISBN: 979-8-9924550-1-4

All rights reserved. No portion of this book may be
reproduced in any form without permission from
the publisher, except as permitted by U.S. copyright law.

Cover design by Catherine Weiss

Edited by Jill Boger and Josh Savory

www.gameoverbooks.com

For my parents,
who taught me how to love
and be loved.

The Eucalypts

I. THE DAYDREAM PLACE

II. VACANCIES

III. LIME RIDGE

IV. CAPACITY

Clarity at Hudson River

When the city floods can I meet you here:
      Cold Spring's arched church,
black hawk dipping on currents of crisp

      wind, quiet enough to hear the snow
creaking? At dusk a train will weave along
      the water; its eerie keening

will echo against the hills, a strange
      whalesong I've never heard
before. We'll go silent

      for long minutes as dozens of cars
trail around the corner, filling the river
      valley with one chilling, insistent question.

And if the answer isn't yes, it's no.

I

THE DAYDREAM PLACE

The Daydream Place

1

If we talk about this
you shouldn't confuse my daydreams
with what was really real.

The thin, milky sunlight that morning,
a light sea-breeze pushed Jack's hair back.
He laughed like dashing horses, wildly.

That other woman,
this other man, as solid as a few
ghostly barnswallows.

The voice from that previously locked room —
(cooed softly, echoing, an answer, a trick) —
is a soothing hallucination.

I'll tell you what I can, but
you need to know
that place is not a real place.

2

Jack is younger now.
His eyes needful, too conscious —
they remind me of way back
when he met me.

I forgot to breathe.
We wondered what was going
to happen, lay in the hills
not believing the sunset.

That might just be my memory:
tasting like the best wine,
soft rain. A particular green
freshness, a flare of warmth.

How do you know it doesn't
mean anything? I moved to Texas but I
never got any farther away.

3

It started in the middle
of the night, when we lived
on a fault-line in California.

The ground rolled, pulling free,
like a cliff or a mountain falling far
away, deep shaking at the other end of a tunnel.

Where do you go? It all came down:
the moonlight, the bottle,
a cindery white cloud.

I groped for my clothes,
tipping off the bedspring, fingers
closing on a wadded pair of socks.

Jack began to laugh, crazily.
He held on to me, waiting
for whatever would happen next.

4

Maybe something could have been
done. Maybe not. Jack seemed smaller
holding the green bottle,
his eyes unfocussed, darker.

I had a need without a name:
blackberries in September,
indigo blackberries wild and tangled,
that restless clarity.

The ocean was still there
but nothing changed.
It was not just once
telling him to lay off.

Jack wanted most to hurt himself.
I don't even think he knew
how to be healthy. Of course,
that wasn't my responsibility.

Jack swallowed an aspirin
and turned toward that smooth
bottle as if he had never
tasted anything so fine.

5

You can't have everything
you want. Not the glitter
of the city and the Milky Way.
I was a girl building shrines
from sycamore twigs, under opaque

skies. Asking Aphrodite to be loved
back. The hammock's taut cords
stretched a tenuous balance;
suspended us without
tipping. Daily, I chose precarity.

The diffuse orange
luminescence of our many
lamps may confuse the song birds,
who keep waiting for true
darkness. But there's Polaris —

6

I am urgent with memories:
tugging at Jack's belt buckle, teeth
in his skin, a blaze of light.
I would not be satisfied. Pulled him
into me with animal yearning, low voice
softly crying out, crisp smell
of his close pores, hips, shoulder,
knees. I saw in his eyes
some wonderful fury
like rain at night, lightning
at the horizon.   That bright,
remembered morning burned
into my heart. Jack wondered about his capacity
to handle something so visceral.
It was hard for anybody to handle.
My coming was no small urgency —
we could conceal the stars.

7

He got angry with me
when I said, *You can't see Orion
in summer*; insisted he had.

One August night, when I
was young, a park ranger pointed
the white beam of his flash

light at the dark parking lot
pavement when I asked
him where Orion was.

Our hot sky blazes with Aquila,
Pegasus, Sagittarius; what he saw
was just any three stars.

8

Apollo gave Cassandra the ability to see
the future, but when she refused to marry
him he cursed her never to be believed:
Ever since that fault I could persuade
no one of anything.

A girl sails off the coast
of Greenland, two braids whipping
in cold sea mist. She persuades
me. My body keeps time
to the world's decay.

My professor said Shakespeare's women
understand time better
than the men, know it in their bodies.
There are deadlines to my desires;
I know it when the blood sheds.

9

I thought it was my job
to make him feel better.
To protect him — like a little
boy, his lips trembling.
He didn't even like it.
But he liked the fall,

that feeling of unreality
smelling like hay, straw,
pulling a muddy radish
out of the damp
and weedy ground,
dull gold sun on the western road.

Jack entered
the clarity of dark woods at
the rim of the forest.
He knew when the end came,
turned the other way,
would not look back.

10

I'm being sorry for myself.
I look back each time
I hear his voice.
I can't help looking.
I don't want to go.

11

I'm coming back to the place I left behind:
northern California, the moon on the ocean,
piney scent, salty tang of nostalgia.

Jack found a feeling of cleanness and health.
He remembered fruit trees, calling birds.
I was not expecting him to feel better.

I'm glad — he's safer now. But I think we're close
to some sort of end. A connection to this place
and the place from which we set out.

12

I had trusted him to return,
knew he had enough strength

to answer the requirements
of the particular moment:

this fluid fabric of gray-golden light
pooled across the room.

Jack inhaled, his nutlike eyes softening.
How do you feel, Jack?

For the first time in his adult life
he said *good*, lit with an emotional

radiance, autumnal and lonely.
He had come to realize

he could be a part of life's rapture
anytime he wanted —

every day a little longer, no rush,
no such thing as too much light.

13

I meet myself in a dream
and though I'm wearing
a different body,
we laugh with recognition.

I ask her what should I do?
She doesn't know.
Everyone in this
dream doesn't know.

What kind of a dream
is that? No answers
no revelations.

Before we met
I dreamt I lived in Santa Fe
and finally felt at home again
in a place I've never been:

blue sky backdropping
hot orange adobe houses,
red mesas flecked with scrub
brush. I woke up craving

desert isolation, prickling
arid breeze, that feeling
of rightness I'm still
not sure exists.

14

If I had dreamed he would
go clean, stop drinking, gradually

grasp that good, fresh apple feeling,
I might have been tempted to stay.

15

Can I really never go back
to the smell of ocean salt,
evergreens in great open fields,
now as it should be, with new sanity?

16

A friend tags him
in a photo: atop a fire
watch tower, snowy
woods and hills
spread around him.

Leaning relaxed, one
arm propped up on the
railing. Century-old relic
of when rangers scanned
the mountains for smoke.

The afternoon in the picture
looks bright, and very cold.
I don't know who he is
looking at but he looks happier
than I've ever seen him.

17

That day at the lake thick smoke
hung in a rising arc from the fire.

Jack was waking up
to an ocean of grassland,

dizzying breadth of conscious
experience, a feeling he would

have thought impossible. The earth
shifted and settled into a new position.

It was clear he had only ever been
distractedly conscious, but at last

he moved slowly, filled with wonder.
Jack, please be porous, and trembling,

please believe I expected this to happen, please
say something sweet.

Lover as Chaparral

The breeze sweeps
through tall grass
and oxalis the way
I run my fingers
through your hair.

I'm supposed to see
you as something separate
from the hillside, but
your irises reflect
the eucalyptus,
both umber as
the earth beneath you.

We cannot wrench
ourselves from terrain
nor time. A peregrine falcon
rests on the lift
of a thermal column.
Suspended above the trees,
it appears still.
But this hill was formed
from shallow sea sediment,
shells still fossilized
in its boulders. Bay
peoples twined these same
fibrous vines into baskets,
before the mining companies
stripped the land of limestone.
Bayberry Pond dries
and refills each year, seasonal
by restorationist design
to avoid spawning
voracious bullfrogs.

Do I use you as
we've used the ridge—
cherish, consume, try to save?

When the air matches
my body temperature
so perfectly, how can I help
but become the thing
that surrounds you, as
this hill is encased
in atmosphere?
The hummingbird's wings
are too quick to track, so
it hangs motionless
at each scarlet blossom
before vanishing
to appear at the next.

It's taken a long time
to realize we're speaking.
I can't say we sound
like robins or branches
rustling, but I can say
I find our voices
indistinguishable.

You may not believe me;
I hardly believe myself.
The sun shines
through us, not on us, and
I press myself
to you as if to land.

II

VACANCIES

Runoff, Fourth Lake, Adirondacks

It's bad design that joy resides so close
to anxiety in the nervous system.

The lovers entwine so tightly in my mind,
my new lover has to remind me: I'm *happy* —
          I *wanted* this.

I used to wonder what my body had to do with me.
Now I'm teenaged in my hushed lust for him.

I press his hand to my heart in the night,
into the vacancies.

Ace of Cups

Imagine a string of unrelated objects,
perhaps all starting with a letter
of the alphabet. Bird. Bell. Bishop.
Bridge. Boat. Basket. Beaver. Or
Potato. Picnic. Pocket. Pea. This rests
the part of the brain that tries
to make sense, a supposed cure
for insomnia. Some nights
I try for hours. I shuffle
the tarot deck to see what comes next.
Lately good news: rainbows,
chariots, lions, rivers. For the first
time he leaves his toothbrush here. What if
there's a happy ending after all?
Water enough to overflow the cup?
My best hope is that we can't tell
the future. Maybe this year rain will fill
the reservoirs. What color are your eyes? he asks.
I'd believe him if he said they were golden.

Waiting Song

The sea flows the way I don't,
though I am meant to mimic
its tides, their swell and ebb,
as the moon clothes and
unclothes herself. I am late.
More than a week. I bite
my cuticles until they bleed.

The last boy was a drummer
with blisters on his fingers.
Should I call them men
now that they pose this threat?
He was playful but he was not
gentle. Often they touch like
the thing they love best: paint
on a palette, a vibrating string,
computer keys, scalpel.

The sea rises the way it shouldn't.
They don't consider themselves
responsible. I attend my pulse, shovel
sand over my feet;
the mound grows and grains
trickle back to the beach.
Waves roll a pirate's shanty
I've known since girlhood:
A drop of Nelson's blood
wouldn't do us any harm
A night with the girls
wouldn't do us any harm.

OK Cupid Profile

I grew up on a dairy farm in upstate New York.

I imagine a childhood
so unlike my seasonless suburban fog:
cattle grazing in the paddock,
he'd carry water to the herd on humid nights,
fall asleep to their lowing, fold his fingers
around an udder, tug until the hot milk
rang in the pail. Once he saw a calf
being born — his father reached an arm
to the elbow into the cow and pulled
her out, slick and squirming.

Just one of those daydreams. Of course
the cows lined up in the milking parlor,
kept in precise cycles of gestation
and lactation. Methane expelled
from their intestines or rose off the surface
of manure lagoons. Autumns lost days
to longer summers. He couldn't hear
their calls from his bedroom
any better than I could.

A Child is Asleep

I was born on a fault line. Two earthquakes shook my mother's labor. Dad read Laura Ingalls Wilder aloud at bedtime so I would dream of sod houses and oranges. Teaching me to coast on two wheels, he pushed my bike, riderless, *see how it wants to stay up?* A barn owl roosted in the palm tree next door; I picked through his pellets for mouse skeletons, sometimes caught his white shadow cutting through the black sky. Neighbor kid held aloft a mangled crawdad corpse, screaming I'd stepped on it. What did I know of danger? All summer, imagination games transformed our street into a maze of treachery — driveways ponds of ice, lawns plunging canyons, red beds of decorative California rock pits of lava. Illicit magic of the muddy creek beyond the barbed wire sign: PRIVATE PROPERTY. What does any endangered species know? In my latchkey-kid afternoons I tried to worship ancient gods at makeshift altars. Hours in the fruitless mulberry's notched branches, milky juice oozing from its broken stems, licking nectar from honeysuckles I tore off the schoolyard's chain link fence. One night I sat up alone at the sliding glass door, entranced as I watched the world exist without us: a family of raccoons cavorted in a raucous circus through our dark backyard.

The life I have

is three blocks away from
the life I want: tall elms loom
over my aimless walks down
Ladd's Addition's planned diagonals.
July roses, outline of a child's body
in chalk next to the hopscotch squares
like a crime scene of happiness.

I want to cordon off the whole
neighborhood, collect pavement DNA,
count leaves and petals. Interrogate
witnesses: neighbors who inoculate
trees against disease each year, monitor
tops of foliage for wilting. Demand they confess
everything they know that I don't:
>How did this happen?
>How can I trace the line
>between now and that porch swing
>in the shade, craftsman, Tudor, baby
>laughing with his mother, silhouette
>of tiny fingers on the sidewalk?

I only know it didn't happen
naturally; never emerge where I expect.

Condensation, Hawthorne Boulevard

At the café I clear tables, nest
water cups until they form a fragile

tower leaning towards me.
Stormlight shifts through the clouds

in brief bursts of glare,
glints off glass and disappears.

A. walks in from the early spring
showers; it's as if I've conjured him

from the density of fog.
I thought of him and he *materialized,*

shoulders broad in a grey shirt,
all warm, all here, and I am here

though I feel sometimes like I'm flickering
against a gust of air.

—

April nights we move
from one streetlamp glow to the next.

Soon these pools of light will warm into islands
of heat, not enough trees to cool

the city. Our elm-lined streets are safe
for now, but the air stagnates around us.

I cling to his arm.
A hanging branch

against my cheek, summer
sharpening its claws.

—

We buy cheap moscato
and sparkling cherry limeade.

The spritzes are flat pink
and sour. If I wanted,

I could sit across from him as long
as the rain keeps filling the reservoir.

Bottle of merlot over a chessboard
one night in our noiseless house.

We toast the supposed future.
His trusting eyes look up at me.

The thought of the rest of my life
opposite this man, and that look.

—

With him I get still;
alone I'm needy,

making tea in the middle of the
night. An urge

to cut triangles from colored paper,
to fold origami or put together a puzzle.

I can't tell if peace is preferable.
Footfalls echo through the ceiling

as my neighbor settles his daughters
for sleep. The door to my apartment building

slams closed. Only the swish of water
under car tires tells me it's still raining.

—

Sometimes I know his touch
when he's almost forgotten it.

He traces his fingers
up and down my shoulder

in slow, clockwise circles,
idle, almost accidental,

almost the way he'd touch
his own body.

He finds the bruise I got
lifting chairs onto tables,

a coffee stain breaking through.
I cover it with his fingertip, then press.

—

I like the city skyline best
from the window above his headboard.

When he's between my knees
I grip the edge

and watch the lamps blink on
the first warm night of the year.

From here, I can't see
what's already burning.

Sirens, drunken voices,
magnolia blossom breeze

ease through the window screen.
I float towards the hill

dotted with yellow lights —
here, not here; with him and not.

Clarity at Tanglewood North

There are times to wait, to do
          nothing. Late August nights in Austin,
A. would walk me around in the apartment

          pool. Water still warm
from the just bearably brutal afternoon
          sun. Cicadas with their mechanical

sibilations, chlorinated close
          darkness, liquid plash in the filters
as he carried me

          through the shallow end. I thought I could convince
myself there was nothing
          but him. An airless summer,

and nowhere else to go.

Clarity at Washougal River

The Cascades Chinook's *rushing water* can still
        in temporary pools — cold, green cues
to pause. Harder than it sounds:

        climb down the slippery rock
face, swift current drags at my ankles
        moss on fallen logs, a day of balance, of trying

not to fall. I'm learning anger is better
        than despair. Found the six pack of tallboys he'd hidden
in a pile of laundry. Four already missing.

        A ghost shouts *timber* from the woods, crashing
giants felled for lumber. Growth takes ages;
        killing is quick.

I pile up my losses and they stack impressively.
        Come home and it's still light. A revelation
of brightness, longer days. I keep repeating

        myself. Who cares about light.

Turbidity at Barton Springs

Is it time to go?
No, I've made my choice:
voice of the grackle, frigid pool,
school of rapid fish, agile —
fragile ferny structures quaking,
breaking surface ripples. Mild,
wild glance of air,
though heat normally chokes,
coaxes a lungless salamander from her nest,
testing the warm water. Slippery minnow
winnow through nooks unlit,
sunlit branches dip and skim,
rim the waterline. Here he is:
his back to me.
He is a name I know.
Low, resonant,
present. Within my reach,
speech extrinsic. Sometimes I
try to need him more,
adore the surprise of him, though
no part's opaque.
Lake up to his chin now,
how easily he knows what to do.

The Rivers and the Lakes

Sometimes when I get anxious I Google *waterfalls*, click play on that TLC song, then on Images. All too fake, neon pink rainbows, Photoshopped lens flare. I add *oregon* to my search for a more familiar gray. It actually helps to see them plummeting but still. I'm getting better at calming myself down. I still feel like something bad is going to happen, tell A. to be careful. When he goes to buy me eggs I list the risks: sidewalkless streets, 105-degree heat, concealed carry laws, police eager to aim. His family didn't immigrate: Texas came to them. But I'm the one who moved us here. Streetlights go dark when the power grid fails us. I keep finding dead birds, like this place isn't able to keep anything alive. When I repeat the list to my therapist, he tells me to think of myself as a lake of unknown depth, cold and dark as you descend, roiling with life: slow trout, slick tadpoles, miniature water insects. But along the surface an opulent glitter — the sun glances like a thousand skipped stones. He leans a little heavy on metaphor. He helps but it helps more to imagine the water cascading, endlessly, with no one there to photograph it.

#shesaidyes

Beachlight or Instagram filters
wash out their faces,

outlines blurred in overexposed
whiteness; can't see the divisions.

I want to. I hope
they're not so whole as that.

Do they think of the shoreline
inching closer with each anniversary?

I've been trying
hard to live right.

I drink big bottles of water.
I do yoga. The spinal twists

wring the air right out
of me, those tight breaths

I gasp when I'm anxious.
I unfurl to fill back up.

I try to learn the names of Texas
trees: live oak, redbud, cedar elm.

I recycle my aluminum,
vote blue. Still, sweating horror

melts into the very courthouse
where they'll tie the knot.

After the hot shower pricks
my skin pink, I turn

the tap to cold
so my blood leaps.

I wonder, to be whole
and vigorous enough to love you

do I have to be one of those
insufferable people

who wake up early
and only drink green tea?

How good do I have to be
to save us?

Sometimes I think
it shouldn't be this hard

but I have dreams
where I can't tie my shoes.

Nights I forget to be
in love. My phone erupts

with executive orders.
I try to believe

as much as they do
in a future.

Your Sister-in-Law is Pregnant in Los Angeles

It's obvious now; strangers
offer their seats on the tram
up the hill to the Getty.

She waves them off,
flashes a white smile,
keeps her body's secrets.

As though what she carries
is something abstract — not a small animal
who already urinates, masturbates, cries.

Too unpretty to consider. Smog swells
over the city. You ask
what's it like? So tender. I wish

I could ask more: does it hurt?
what rain will water its growing?
When will it be my turn; what world

will be left when it is? To answer
you she skims the surface
of sensation: a sanitized description

of sleeker hair, thicker nails, but
one detail tantalizes me:
she dreams more vividly.

In the privacy of her body,
her baby also dreams.

Clarity at Russian River

The bathing suit I'd borrowed didn't fit.
    Wet polyester crawled into the fold
under my breasts, too tight and too loose

    at once. Slick river rocks slid beneath my feet
and the barbeque burned.
    Watched him talking on the shore.

Hated him some for bringing me
    like an offering out
into the loud sun and talk

    of strangers. Swam upstream
to spite him, leave him
    wondering where I'd gone.

Drought made the current
    mellow. I floated back
down on the surface,

    belly up, arms open, ears underwater.

Bride Series

for Buttercup

as though those
were the most important
words — a three-letter
contract of devotion —
I do

           I do — if you didn't
           say it you didn't do
           it — you didn't
           find your white horse
           in time

farm boy finds
a summer home of
unexpected fire —
hands her a pitcher —

           she's calm deciding
           death is preferable to his absence—
           last recourse of the hopeless
           — stays for true love —
           a kissing book

it is — I do —
a kissing book with
another important word —
putrescence

           a preoccupation with pain —
           as though you could meter
           pain — as you wish — death
           too a matter of degrees

mostly dead is still
slightly alive —
it would take a miracle

                              I learned the remedy
                              for distress is cold
                              water — witch in my head
                              screaming accusations:

queen of refuse
— queen of putrescence

                              I do recognize the coughing
                              punctuated music —
                              true love — mostly dead — kissing
                              book — putrescence — I do

Time Lapse of Eagle Creek, Columbia Gorge

Fire pours through the canyon,
day to night to day, an errant
firework ignites the thirty-
one second inferno.

We visited those woods years
ago. That night I couldn't sleep;
he sat up with me talking
in the cool darkness.

When dawn blazed green
in the canopy and fog glowed
pearly silver against the window
I turned away from him to finally rest.

—

So is it wrong, now, to walk the edges
of a crowded faraway island,
sea breeze slipping through
my empty fingertips,

bubbling with joy at children
diving below waves, Ferris wheel
soaring into blue? Wrong
to love my loneliness and freedom

so ferociously as he writes:
this morning he swept
ash from his mother's windowsill
and missed me?

Stories and Feed

My hair stylist had a baby;
moved to Ohio, learned

floral design, for months
she posted Instagram photos:

her rounding belly strewn
with flowers, pollen on her nose,

flushed cheeks she named
a florist's blush. She grew

her hair long. Now it's the small
body of the boy who appears

illuminated in my palm daily
for ten seconds or less,

asleep in a sunbeam, fist curled
in a loose ball above his head,

dust motes casting miniature
rainbows on his brow.

I tap a tiny circle
and my iPhone blooms

with this cosseted infant and his
mother, who wanted him so acutely

she chose to carry him through
every uncertainty alone.

So now when I envision
my son he's drowsing

in the pillowy center of a large duvet,
coverlet ridges rippled around him —

I lay him down
again and again

in this imaginary bed
and you're never there.

The Tree with the Lights in It

The vision comes and goes, mostly goes, but I live for it…
—Annie Dillard, *Pilgrim at Tinker Creek*

I'm looking for the white ponderosa
I saw in a stand of evergreens
the night before I left Oregon.

The white pine
not sagging with snowdrift
but shining, or shined upon,
every needle
branch, bark,
roots as though buried
white. All of it seen,

me seeing
all of it

and seen, too.

I felt only
gratitude

and an instinct
to protect.

III

LIME RIDGE

Four Views of the Brooklyn Botanic Garden

1

Years later Jack visits me in New York.
We're surprised to recognize
the plants in the Warm Temperate Pavilion;
controlled climate transports
us to the California streets of our
suburban childhoods: birds
of paradise, gladioli, poppies
we were taught never to pluck but
he harvested from neighbors'
yards for homebrew opium. Iris
the electric blue he once saw
in a dream and described
as his favorite color. I was eighteen
then, not yet all the way
in love with him.
My favorite color is blue too,
I said as we walked
around and around the plaza.

2

Every echinacea reminds
me of him: bright tips of paleae
arranged fractally to draw my gaze
to the dark center. I like
when I open a door and
he's behind it.

3

On the subway I poise
the paper-coned stem
of lilies he bought me.
Their mild fragrance
the whole ride home.
This is the small
version of how he left me
the first time.

4

The greenhouse bonsai trees,
miniature replicas
of the giants, were believed more
potent when smaller. Roots
cramped in containers, tiny red
leaves I wanted to touch
but couldn't. Every replanting,
ever more distorted.

The train doors close
behind him and
I'm not as relieved
as I should be.

Precipitation, Prospect Lefferts Gardens

In the fourth month the magnolia
on my morning walk
to the subway is in pink riot.
The cupped, white-edged petals
absorb cool sunshine
that shifts,
suddenly, some afternoons,
to squalling thunder
and hail. I am turning
twenty-nine beneath
its branches, resisting
the incessant hunch
that there's something
I should have done by now.

Scientists say we have a dozen
years to cut emissions; I might
have as many to conceive.
The last man told me
maybe in three years, then
he took it back. I count
them like the hours
between dusk and dawn
but no one will tell
me how much time
is left. Days lengthen,
shorten. What I want relies
on this: a spring that will return,
my body with its fragile
and unknown interior.

Yesterday a man fell
into the empty tracks.
Shouts rang along the platform
as we pulled him to safety.
But his open hand reminded me:
some of us get stuck, reaching.

Boxing Day: Lime Ridge

the trouble is I never let go of anything
not the red and teal crumpled wrapping

      not the day we walked up this hill
with champagne shoved in Jack's bag

all week I've been ten places at once
but never here   his cat knocked her jaw

on my cheek and time collapsed
like a telescope   tomorrow and two

years ago   an aerial glance at dry fields
before the fog closes over   two hundred

years ago   only forests   ten
twenty years from now   only wasteland

land keeps its burn cycles   I keep
leaving   mostly California

but today   my mom's too large fleece sweater
boots wrested from a closet shelf

limestone miners climbed the same
steep hill   I lose my breath

      we checked that tree for figs
all summer but found only hard

small fruit   or at night trying
to see all the sky at once to catch

the Perseids   my eighteenth summer all
smoke   dirt splits in the sun   my state

golden but too dry and on fire
        eucalyptus resin smells the same

but I remember a man who still
feels new   the cracks in us

could have been   fractures or hatching
stretch marks on a growing body

Rain Lilies, Austin, Texas

They budge out of soil, pointed
white tips tall on spindle stems,
soaked in summer showers so
unlike my hometown dry season.

I've never seen them but here
they are, stark on the road verge,
alien starbursts on a naked stem,
urgent along their bare uprightness.

Starry petals sharp
on my fingertips just by looking,
they arrive without warning, native
to this city of humid unbelonging.

But here I'm always startled:
cicadas scream from trees,
a grackle dive-bombs, protecting
her nest, claws in my hair.

I miss my old problems. At least
arid grassland primed to blaze
at every flicked cigarette
is a devil I know.

The flowers stand mockingly erect.
At once I want to gather the snowy
origami blossoms into bright, rigid
bundles and crumple them under my boot.

I ache to grip their purity, and
I can't stand their white hearts.

Clarity at Lake Merritt

For the first time I ask
> if you're seeing anyone.
Lake Merritt catches

> late afternoon light. You say no.
My breath catches
> across the water. Cheerful

music thumps:
> an engagement party,
balloon bride and groom,

> two balloon rings interlocked.
A cormorant struggles
> with a flat silver fish

flashing like plastic trash.
> You say you couldn't
when you were so tired.

> The cormorant dives. I say
I liked being with you even
> when you were tired.

We were always best
> in the damp grass. The fish thrashes.
The bride snaps her ribbon

> tether and lurches into the sky.

As Easy as That

What is it, Katie asked, *You poke holes*
in the Big Dipper's cup and it pours
on the lion's head? We hugged in the middle
of the street and when Chris said,
Goodnight, kid, I felt a high, thin longing
in the back of my skull. Glanced
between the blinds of a basement apartment,
tussled and dark-haired, the neighbor
boy slept with the lights on.
A lover's vision, him flushed,
still in the summer night.

In Portland the air never cooled
with the sinking sun. I was awake
all night; stalked my apartment
wearing next to nothing, pressed
a water glass to my temple, condensation
dripping down my jaw.
I lay under the breeze
of the ceiling fan and sensed
the spaces and losses.
Summer insists upon absences,
spreads truth out flat, wavering. That year
the city warmed up too fast; rhododendrons
all died on their stems. What else
will shrivel before I find
what my friends have found?

But when I pressed the button
the elevator came to me as it
came to the boy in the bed.
And I had to remind myself
how easy it all still was, how sweet

sometimes, bushes blushing green, breeze as
mild as the first day you feel healthy
after a cold, body a revelation, how
could you always feel like this
and never notice? The freshness
of cherries in your mouth, the wondrous
fact that there are cherries,
and that you can eat them.

I felt like the sound of a harp

It was two years before we fell in love before the lightning before the fires I was bored at the party because my first boyfriend was ignoring me I wandered into the bedroom Jack was there with two of our friends they all had balloons in their hands pinching the tops to keep the (compressed) gas from escaping he invited me to do one I asked what is it Kristen said nitrous oxide, like at the dentist I said sure okay there was a loud pop when he emptied a canister into the balloon for me I took it I think it was blue he told me to breathe in and out into it the gas had a chemical sweetness like vanilla extract I let go of the balloon (short term decrease in manual dexterity) but I don't remember that (short term decrease in mental performance) I couldn't think anymore (derealization) someone was laughing it was me laughing (euphoria, depersonalization, sound distortion) I took big breaths of real air (diffusion hypoxia) then just like that it was over I felt so lonely I thought I was going to cry but Jack saw me get quiet he sat with me he said it's okay not for the last time I believed him.

Percolation, Ygnacio Valley

My first boyfriend sneaked me through
the unlatched gate as August
afternoon drained into evening.
Perched on his lap; a thin t-shirt
loose over my swimsuit
dampened two circles at my
breasts. Breath trickling
into my ear: when I lifted myself
from the water, he said he saw
the strands of dark new hair
peeking from the edge of my bikini
and it thrilled him. Too bashful
to lift his head from mine,
he hid his face in my neck.
But I tilted my chin up, tips
of my toes grazing the patio,
his warm thighs under mine,
new fiery flush of desire
rising in my adolescent blood,
to watch the blushing sky,
eager for the first bright pinpricks
that announce the advancing darkness.

Event Horizon, April

We have seen what we thought
was unseeable. The amorphous
orange-rimmed disk pulsates
on my computer screen like a breathing
thing. But no, it's a trick
of the eye, my eye, unable to absorb
this *part of the universe that was*
off limits to us, making the glowing
orb shift and throb. The black hole is
55 million light-years away. Carbon dioxide
will climb to 500 parts
per million in 50 years.
I can't see that far —

so I don't know what it means
to be *able to actually see*
this shadow and to detect it,
that the ocular ring *gives a glimpse*
of what the future might hold,
but it doesn't give us all
the information that we want.
I stare at this place where time
stands still, as if standing at
the mouth of a cave, maw
of a pit, cusp of a choice.
Horror of unseen danger
and the impulse to enter.

Clarity at Sacramento River

Our friends married in the hot valley
            but we sat at separate tables.
Sometime after toasts I must

            have asked you to come
outside with me to sit by the pool.
            The water glowed its green, still cradle

for the July moon; a circle
            of lamplight enclosed us but shadowed
your eyes. It was nothing like

            that afternoon on the hill
in the dry eucalyptus casings when I closed
            and opened my eyes

to see you newly. We knew
            what the problems would be
and did nothing.

            Music floated our friends' laughter
through the windows as I turned to face
            an orchard of almond trees

heavy with fruit in the scorched
            fields. A vista wide
enough to get lost in

            but not nearly enough to sustain me.

California was not always called that.

Once it was known the wild lands.

imagine how you would feel if you had to admit that you lived on So changed.

When I think of California

it's not golden hills or sprays of poppies
fiery orange at sunset,
misty redwoods and salamanders
seeping out of moist earth, oranges
hanging full on the neighbor's tree,
suction of icy waves sinking my feet into sand,
zipping through the Caldecott Tunnel
at dusk, windows down, stereo up,
on my way to a party in the city
where I will stand outside at midnight
and the sky will be clear for once, deck
still warm under my bare feet, trying
to understand how a place so alive
could be so dying, suffocated,
parched, more fire acres
each year, only ash raining until flash
floods erode the coast, and I have no idea
how to save it, or how your
laugh will bring me back to the cold
drink in my hand, or how
the fog will still roll over the hills
in the morning that I miss. It's
your eucalyptus eyes and how
they brightened in sunlight
the summer we searched for figs.

Evaporation, Mount Lassen

I touch the mountain
each year believing I've changed
and it hasn't. Snowy or
scorched, its summit etches
the same line in me.
But the lava dome
is active; a seismograph
needle traces
its every tremble.
A mudpot spews sulfur, scalding
spring erodes rock. The conifer
burns, grows back; manzanita
needs heat to seed but fire
intervals keep getting
shorter. Willow roots show
how high Butte waters used to be.
Hat Creek becomes Hat Lake
when the beavers dam it,
and becomes a meadow
when they move on.

IV

CAPACITY

Ode to Empire

The night greenhouse
of the Brooklyn Botanic Garden
glows a purple
patch of otherworldly
light on the new
snow. It takes me
by surprise — as if
even the moon
were different here.

This city stands
for me as it has
for others for liberty.
Salt wind in my
hands at Coney Island,
golden steeple blinks
over another building's
flat blue top.
On my birthday
I find a perfect
pair of shoes, my size,
green snake skin
kitten heels
with a pointed toe,
in the foyer of my
apartment building.

These are the moments
of perfection I wanted.
Vespertine scents
of New York: cold air,
human bodies, chestnuts
cooking in carts.
Tonight has a hot heart;
my footsteps pulse
to the subway.

Sky stopped up with orange
fog but there are things
better than stars:
stoplights flipping green,
glinting gutter ice.

Here I'm always walking
toward something, as
sirens spiral away
to some other disaster.

There are rules I take
pleasure in following.
Stand to the right,
walk to the left.
This applies to escalators
and moving walkways
of all sorts. At certain
restaurants you will need
to write your name
on a slip of paper, take
a ticket, wait
in two lines.
Regardless, you must
know what you want
before you're asked. Instead
of craning your neck
to marvel at the skyscrapers'
apex, angle your gaze
from a distance.

A short history
of places I've
made out in New York:
Lying in the grass
in Prospect Park.

The top of the stairs
of the Jay St.
Metrotech subway
stop. Penn Station
as several trains
came and went.
Stoplight at Broadway
and 79th. Stoplight
at Bergen and Bedford.

I forgot what it was
like to love him,
a form of amnesia.
Something happened
that I didn't expect:
it was okay.

Keep moving.
Remember how wide
the radius of your umbrella
sits; if you approach
someone without an umbrella,
lift yours up so they
can walk beneath and
past. Don't get into an Uber
unless you know
for sure it's yours.

Of course, some moments
are demoralizing. Forgetting
laundry detergent, two blocks back
to the apartment, wind
blows frozen trash
around my feet, rats
scuttle under dumpsters,

odors of feces and gasoline
fume from the sewer grates.
The laundromat plays
the news all day; a pipeline
bursts, coats grasslands
in oil. Shirts stitched
in sweatshops or prisons
churn circles behind
glass portholes.

I asked this morning,
Is there any good news?
My new lover
said no. The last
rhinoceros died. They kept
saying that, but
it was the last male.
Two females burdened
saviors of the subspecies.
And that was not
even the worst of it.

The funny thing is,
I'm not sad. I think
I'm stumbling toward a joy
so tenacious
it exists upside-down.

That reminds me,
be careful on first dates
or you may fall in love
with how he combs
his fingers through his hair
giving himself
little boy bedhead.

Or how when he's thinking
and talking at the same
time he closes his eyes.
A conspiratorial arch
of the eyebrow could
capture you, especially if,
side by side at the
bar, he laughs
at your joke, touches your wrist.

Here I want to fuck
everyone, all the time.
We say *thirsty* now,
I say *I'm thirsty*
the way wheat fields thirst
for summer lightning.
Passerby shadows
through the opaque
window glass. I keep
waiting for it to get
old, when will I want
what I always thought
I'd want? I want it
less than ever.

Crying is absolutely
permissible in all
public locations.
If you feel faint
on a crowded rush hour
train, ask to sit
and someone
will stand for you.

Now I carry gum
in my purse. Now
I have a pocket
for my MetroCard
and nothing else
goes in that pocket.
Now I can walk
forever. Anymore,
I don't gasp
breaths sharp
and anxious that
make my chest hurt,
even when I drink

too much coffee, even
when exhaust fumes fill
my nostrils, even when
my phone says
the weather is smoke,
my lungs swell
for their next, for
whatever comes next.

Adaptive Capacity

First April Sunday, I help
Claire in her garden.
We puzzle over soil mixes,
new at growing what will
someday feed us.

In the kitchen I write
plant labels on popsicle sticks
to differentiate the rows
of tender green shoots
from one another. Claire
crouches beside the raised
planter boxes. Her attention
set to the most delicately
beckoning vegetable finger
soothes, if only for a moment,
that tightness in her chest
from reading the scientific
papers: foliage browns from lack
of water vapor, bees
vanish, monarchs lose
migrational direction in
erratic waves of hot and cold.

Last Friday she took me to synagogue;
we remembered the temples
destroyed, rebuilt, destroyed.
White hairs in her dark curls prove
it's been a long time since
we laughed at the first tree
to drop all its needles. Grownups
now, but she doesn't want
a baby anymore. Too much
carbon in his tiny breaths.

Instead she's my deity of spring:
her greenery sponges
up the greenhouse gasses.

It's not as if she forgets
the butterflies whose milkweed
has already withered
in March warmth
when the garden sprouts
its new tendrils. She
will still lose sleep over
the shrinking coral reef.
But at least there persists
this growing season, mild
showers between polar
vortex and drought.
The roots gain purchase, little
labels herald: PATTY PAN,
BRANDYWINE, BEANS.

NOTES

The Daydream Place
This poem began as a collage-style found poem from the source text *The Talisman* by Stephen King and Peter Straub. Multiple poem sections include only words found in that novel, though never in the same order/ syntax as the original text.

Ace of Cups
The title of this poem is the name of a card in the Minor Arcana of the Rider-Waite Tarot deck. A. E. Waite describes its divinatory meaning as, "house of the true heart, joy, content, abode, nourishment, abundance, fertility; Holy Table, felicity hereof."

Waiting Song
The italicized lines in this poem are from a sea shanty titled "Nelson's Blood" or "We'll Roll the Old Chariot Along."

OK Cupid Profile
The italicized line in this poem is a quote from an anonymous dating profile.

A Child is Asleep
The title of this poem is borrowed from Annie Dillard's memoir *An American Childhood.*

The life I have
Ladd's Addition is a planned residential neighborhood in Portland, Oregon, one of the oldest developments of its kind in the western United States.

The Rivers and the Lakes
The title of this poem is borrowed from the TLC song "Waterfalls."

Time Lapse of Eagle Creek, Columbia Gorge
This poem refers to a YouTube video taken by Oca Hoeflein of the Eagle Creek Fire, posted September 5, 2017.

Golden Coast
This is an erasure-style found poem from the 1936 children's book *Carmen of the Golden Coast* by Madeline Brandeis.

Bride Series
This poem owes its form to Leslie Scalapino's "bum series". The language borrows generously from the 1987 movie *The Princess Bride*.

I felt like the sound of a harp
The title of this poem is a quote from a patient of chemist Humphry Davy in 1800 after inhaling nitrous oxide.

Event Horizon, April
The italicized lines in this poem are from the New York Times article "Darkness Visible, Finally: Astronomers Capture First Ever Image of a Black Hole" by Dennis Overbye, April 10, 2019.

Ode to Empire
On March 19, 2018, the last male northern white rhinoceros died, leaving behind two female individuals to represent the subspecies. His name was Sudan.

Adaptive Capacity
This poem is dedicated to Claire Wasserman.

ACKNOWLEDGMENTS

The following poems from the manuscript have been previously published, sometimes in different forms or with different titles. My deep thanks to the editors who gave these poems their first homes.

"The Daydream Place," Part 7 - *Tipton Poetry Journal*

"Ace of Cups" - *Grasslimb Journal*

"Waiting Song" - *Argot Magazine*

"The life I have" - *Windfall: A Journal of Poetry and Place*

"Clarity at Tanglewood North" - *Grasslimb Journal*

"The Rivers and the Lakes" - *Construction Literary Magazine*

"#shesaidyes" - *Off the Coast*

"The Tree with the Lights in It" - *Existere Journal of Arts & Literature*

"Boxing Day: Lime Ridge" - *Artificium's Horology: A themed collection of short fiction and poetry*

"Clarity at Lake Merritt" - *Quiddity*

"As Easy as That" - *Austin Public Library's Aural Literature Anthology*

"I felt like the sound of a harp" - *The Hollins Critic*

The following poems originally appeared in earlier forms in a crowd-funded, self-published chapbook, *Northern California Lightning Series*. Thank you to the donors who made that project possible, and to Joseph Carlough at Displaced Snail Press for his design, printing, and binding expertise.

"Clarity at Russian River"

"Boxing Day, Lime Ridge"

"Percolation, Ygnacio Valley"

"Clarity at Sacramento River"

"When I think of California"

THANKS

Thank you to Josh Savory, editor-in-chief of Game Over Books for seeing the merit in this book and selecting it for publication. Thanks as well to editor Jill Boger and cover artist Catherine Weiss for their invaluable contributions.

A gracious community of mentors and readers has upheld me through the writing of this collection. Heartfelt thanks to my teachers Mary Szybist, Jerry Harp, Paul Merchant, Elena Rivera, Jeanne Marie Beaumont, and b ferguson. The book found its final form through the generous and thoughtful guidance of Katie Ford, to whom I will always be grateful.

Thanks also to my cohort at the 92Y Unterberg Poetry Center manuscript class for their attentive reading and input, especially Dorothy Neagle and Malcolm Farley, who read the most nascent form of this manuscript. I appreciate the Binders Full of Women and Non-Binary Poets Facebook group and fellow Game Over Books poet Emily Stoddard's Poetry Bulletin for inspiring and comforting me through the process of submitting my work for publication.

I am grateful to my past loves for their patience and generosity when I've chosen to write about our shared lives. Special thanks to Jack Dillon.

Thank you to my first reader and creative companion Tea Ho. Thank you to my greatest support and champion, Nick Johnson.

Last to thank are really the first, my parents, whose love is the defining truth of my life.

Biography

Casey Elizabeth Newbegin (she/her) was born and raised in California. She is the author of the crowdfunded chapbook Northern California Lightning Series and her work has previously appeared in The Hollins Critic, Quiddity, Tipton Poetry Journal, Existere Journal of Arts & Literature, and other journals. She works as a fine art insurance specialist and lives with her wonderful husband Nick, sweet baby son Nolan, and their two cats – the old, giant lovebug Scoresby and the young, mischievous dust gremlin Naxos – in Brooklyn, NY. The Eucalypts is her first collection.

www.ingramcontent.com/pod-product-compliance
Lightning Source LLC
Chambersburg PA
CBHW040126150726

48005CB00015B/2387